FAVORITE PETS
IN CHARTED DESIGNS

Barbara Johansson

DOVER PUBLICATIONS, INC.
New York

Copyright © 1979 by Barbara Johansson
All rights reserved under Pan American and International Copyright Conventions.

Published in Canada by General Publishing Company, Ltd., 30 Lesmill Road, Don Mills, Toronto, Ontario.
Published in the United Kingdom by Constable and Company, Ltd., 10 Orange Street, London WC2H 7EG.

Favorite Pets in Charted Designs is a new work, first published by Dover Publications, Inc., in 1979.

International Standard Book Number: 0-486-23889-X

Manufactured in the United States of America
Dover Publications, Inc.
180 Varick Street
New York, N.Y. 10014

INTRODUCTION

If your pet is as important a member of your household as mine is, a needlework portrait of that pet is certainly as much a symbol of your home as any sampler saying, "Home Sweet Home." This book contains some of my favorite pets rendered as charted designs. They can be worked in needlepoint, counted crossstitch, latch-hooking, crochet, knitting, etc., and used as pictures, pillows or for decorating fabrics, clothes or anything an animal motif will enhance.

Each of the designs has its own color key. The colors, however, are merely suggestions. You should feel free to substitute your own colors for the ones indicated, thereby creating a design which is uniquely yours. If you decide to create a new color scheme, work it out in detail before beginning a project. To give you a good idea of how the finished project will look, put tracing paper over the design in the book and experiment with your own colors on the tracing paper.

All of the designs are plotted on easy to read grids of ten squares to the inch. Bear in mind that the finished piece of needlework will not be the same size as the charted design unless you happen to be working on fabric that has the same number of threads per inch as the chart has squares per inch. To determine how large a finished design will be, divide the number of stitches in the design by the threadcount of the fabric. For example, if a design that is 60 stitches wide by 84 stitches deep is worked on a 14-count cloth, divide 60 stitches by 14 to get 5 and 84 by 14 to get 6; so the worked design will measure 5" × 6". The same design worked on 10-count fabric would measure approximately 6" × 8½". It is also easy to enlarge the overall dimensions of a design by enlarging the background or by adding a border.

The designs can be worked directly onto needlepoint canvas by counting off the correct number of warp and woof squares shown on the chart, each square representing one stitch to be taken on the canvas. If you prefer to put some guidelines on the canvas, make certain that your marking medium is waterproof. Use either non-soluble inks, acrylic paints thinned appropriately with water so as not to clog the holes in the canvas, or oil paints mixed with benzine or turpentine. Felt-tipped pens are very handy, but check the labels carefully because not all felt markers are waterproof. It is a good idea to experiment with any writing materials on a piece of scrap canvas to make certain that all material is waterproof. There is nothing worse than having a bit of ink run onto the needlepoint as you are blocking it.

There are two distinct types of needlepoint canvas: single-mesh and double-mesh. Double-mesh is woven with two horizontal and two vertical threads forming each mesh, whereas single-mesh is woven with one vertical and one horizontal thread forming each mesh. Double-mesh is a very stable canvas on which the threads will stay securely in place as you work. Single-mesh canvas, which is more widely used, is a little easier on the eyes because the spaces are slightly larger.

A tapestry needle with a rounded, blunt tip and an elongated eye is used for needlepoint. The needle should clear the hole in the canvas without spreading the threads. Special yarns which have good twist and are sufficiently heavy to cover the canvas are used for needlepoint.

Although there are over a hundred different needlepoint stitches, the *Tent Stitch* is universally considered to be the needlepoint stitch. The three most familiar versions of Ten Stitch are: Plain Half-Cross Stitch, Continental Stitch and Basket Weave Stitch.

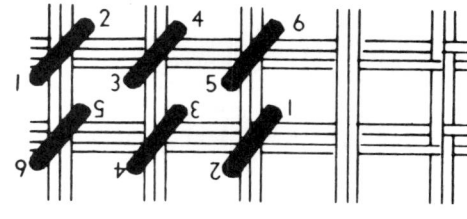

DIAGRAM 1

PLAIN HALF-CROSS STITCH *(diagram 1)*. Always work Half-Cross Stitch from left to right, then turn the canvas around and work the return row, still stitching from left to right. Bring the needle to the front of the canvas at a point that will be the bottom of the first stitch. The needle is in a vertical position when making the stitch. Keep the stitches loose for minimum distortion and good coverage. This stitch must be worked on a double-mesh canvas.

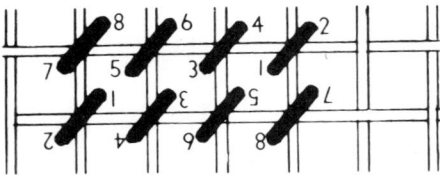

DIAGRAM 2

CONTINENTAL STITCH *(diagram 2)*. Start this design at the upper right-hand corner and work from right to left. The needle is slanted and always brought out a mesh ahead. The resulting stitch is actually a Half-Cross Stitch on top and a slanting stitch on the back. When the row is finished, turn the canvas around and work the return row, still stitching from right to left.

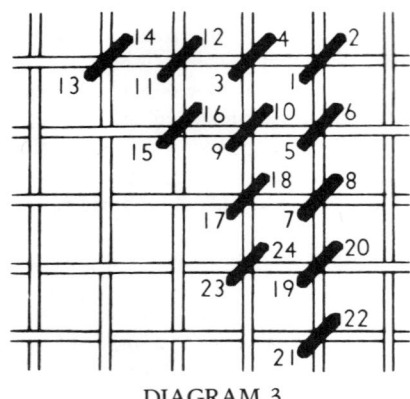

DIAGRAM 3

BASKET WEAVE STITCH *(diagram 3)*. Start in the upper right-hand corner of the area with four Continental Stitches, two worked horizontally across the top and two placed directly below the first stitch. Then work diagonal rows, the first slanting up and across the canvas from right to left and the next down and across from left to right. Each new row is one stitch longer. As you go down the canvas (left to right), the needle is held in a vertical position; as you move in the opposite direction, the needle is horizontal. The rows should interlock, creating a basket-weave pattern on the reverse. If this is not done properly a faint ridge will show where the pattern was interrupted. Always stop working in the middle of a row, rather than at the end, so that you will know in which direction you were working.

Bind all the raw edges of needlepoint canvas with masking tape, double-fold bias tape or even adhesive tape. There are no set rules on where to begin a design. Generally it is easier to begin close to the center and work outward toward the edges of the canvas, working the backgrounds or borders last. To avoid fraying the yarn, work with strands not longer than 18".

When you have finished your needlepoint, it should be blocked. No matter how straight you have kept your work, blocking will give it a professional look.

Any hard, flat surface that you do not mind marring with nail holes and one that will not be warped by wet needlepoint can serve as a blocking board. A large piece of plywood, an old drawing board or an old-fashioned doily blocker are ideal.

Mosten a Turkish towel in cold water and roll the needlepoint in the towel. Leaving the needlepoint in the towel overnight will insure that both the canvas and the yarn are thoroughly and evenly dampened. Do not saturate the needlepoint! Never hold the needlepoint under the faucet as this much water is not necessary.

Mark the desired outline on the blocking board, making sure that the corners are straight. Lay the needlepoint on the blocking board, and tack the canvas with thumbtacks about ½" to ¾" apart. It will probably take a good deal of pulling and tugging to get the needlepoint straight, but do not be afraid of this stress. Leave the canvas on the blocking board until thoroughly dry. Never put an iron on your needlepoint. You cannot successfully block with a steam iron because the needlepoint must dry in the straightened position. You may also have needlepoint blocked professionally. If you have a pillow made, a picture framed, or a chair seat mounted, the craftsman may include the blocking in his price.

These charted designs can also be used for counted cross-stitch. Counted cross-stitch is very simple. The basic ingredients are a small, blunt needle and a fabric that is woven so evenly it appears to be formed in regular blocks or squares. Push the threaded needle up through a hole in the fabric and cross over the thread intersection (or square) diagonally, left to right *(diagram 4)*. This is half the stitch. Now cross back, right to left, making an X.

DIAGRAM 4

One of the great advantages to counted cross-stitch is that the supplies and equipment required are minimal and inexpensive. You will need:

1. A small blunt tapestry needle, #24 or #26.

2. **Evenweave fabric.** This can be linen, cotton, wool or a blend that includes miracle fabrics. The three most popular fabrics are:

Cotton Aida. This is made 14 threads per inch, 11 threads per inch, 8 threads per inch, and so forth. Fourteen, being the prettiest, is preferred.

Evenweave Linen. This also comes in a variety of threads per inch. Working on evenweave linen involves a slightly different technique, which is explained on page vi. Thirty-count linen will give a stitch approximately the same size as 14-count aida.

Hardanger Cloth. This has 22 threads per inch and is available in cotton or linen.

3. **Embroidery thread.** This can be six-strand mercerized cotton floss (DMC, Coats and Clark, Lily, Anchor, etc.), crewel wool, Danish Flower Thread, silken and metal threads or perle cotton. For 14-count aida and 30-count linen, divide six-strand cotton floss and work with only two strands. For more texture, use more thread; for a flatter look, use less thread. Crewel wool is pretty on an evenweave wool fabric, and some embroiderers even use wool on cotton fabric. Danish Flower Thread is a thicker thread with a matt finish, one strand equalling two of cotton floss.

4. **Embroidery hoop.** Use a plastic or wooden 4", 5" or 6" round or oval hoop with a screw type tension adjuster.

5. A pair of sharp embroidery scissors are absolutely essential.

Prepare the fabric by whipping, hemming, or zigzagging on the sewing machine to prevent ravelling at the edges. Next, locate the exact center of the design you have chosen, so that you can then center the design on the piece of fabric. Find the center of the fabric by folding it in half both vertically and horizontally. The center stitch of the design should fall where the creases in the fabric meet.

It's usually not very convenient to begin work with the center stitch itself. As a rule it's better to start at the top of a design, working horizontal rows of a single color, left to right. This technique permits you to go from an unoccupied space to an occupied space (from an empty hole to a filled one), which makes ruffling the floss less likely. To find out where the top of the design should be placed, count squares up from the center of the design, and then count off the corresponding number of holes up from the center of the fabric.

Next, place the section of the fabric to be worked taughtly in the hoop; the tighter the better, for tension makes it easier to push the needle through the holes without piercing the fabric. As you work, use the screw adjuster to tighten as necessary. Keep the screw at the top and out of your way. When beginning, fasten the thread with a waste knot by holding a bit of thread on the underside of the work and anchoring it with the first few stitches *(diagram 5)*. Do all the stitches in the same color in the same row, working left to right and slanting

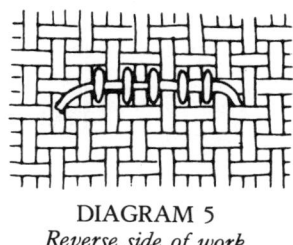

DIAGRAM 5
Reverse side of work

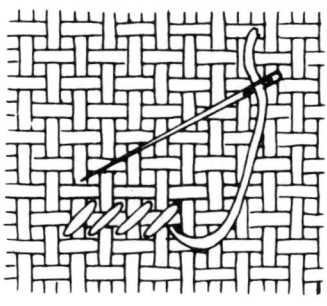

DIAGRAM 6

DIAGRAM 7

DIAGRAM 8

from bottom left to upper right *(diagram 6)*. Then cross back, completing the X's *(diagram 7)*. Some cross-stitchers prefer to cross each stitch as they come to it; this is fine, but be sure the slant is always in the correct direction. Of course, isolated stitches must be crossed as you work them. Vertical stitches are crossed as shown in diagram 8. Holes are used more than once; all stitches "hold hands" unless a space is indicated. The work is always held upright, never turned as for some needlepoint stitches.

When carrying a color from one area to another, wiggle your needle under existing stitches on the underside. Do not carry a color across an open expanse of fabric for more than a few stitches as the thread will be visible from the front.

To end a color, weave in and out of the underside of stitches, perhaps making a scallop stitch or two for extra security *(diagram 9)*. Whenever possible end in the direction in which you are traveling, jumping up a row, if necessary *(diagram 10)*. This prevents holes caused by work being pulled in two directions. Do not make knots; knots make bumps. Cut off the ends of the threads; do not leave any tails because they'll show through when the work is mounted.

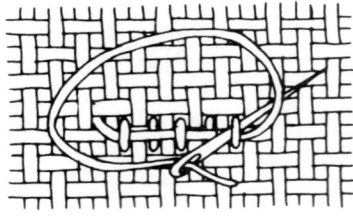

DIAGRAM 9
Reverse side of work

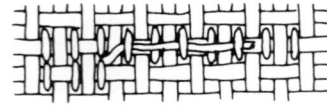

DIAGRAM 10
Reverse side of work

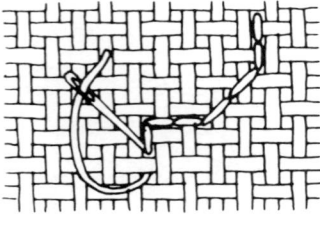

DIAGRAM 11

The only other stitch used in counted cross-stitch is the backstitch. This is worked from hole to hole and may be vertical, horizontal or slanted *(diagram 11)*.

Working on linen requires a slightly different technique. Evenweave linen is remarkably regular, but there are always some thin threads and some that are nubbier or fatter than others. To even these out and to make a stitch that is easy to see, the cross-stitch is worked over two threads each way. The "square" you are covering is thus 4 threads *(diagram 12)*. The first few stitches on linen are sometimes difficult, but one quickly begins "to see in two's." After the third stitch, a pattern is established, and should you inadvertently cross over three threads instead of four, the difference in slant will make it immediately apparent that you have erred.

DIAGRAM 12

Linen evenweave fabric should be worked with the selvage at the side, not at the top and bottom.

Because you go over more threads, linen affords more variations in stitches, A half stitch can slant in either direction and is uncrossed. A three-fourths stitch is shown in diagram 13. Diagram 14 shows backstitch on linen.

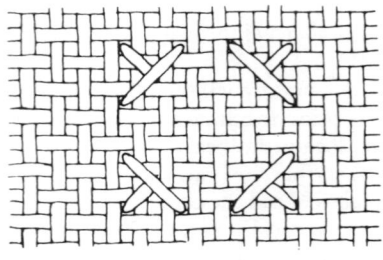

DIAGRAM 13

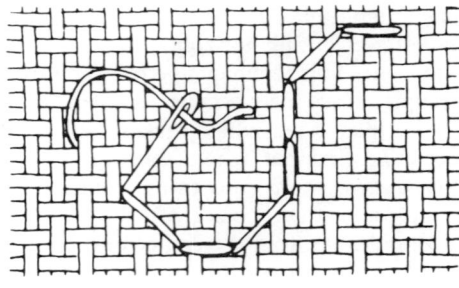

DIAGRAM 14

Gingham or other checkered material can also be used for counted cross-stitch by making the crosses over the checks from corner to corner. If you wish to embroider a cross-stitch design onto a fabric which does not have an evenweave, baste a lightweight Penelope canvas to the fabric. The design can then be worked from the chart by making crosses over the double mesh of the canvas, being careful not to catch the threads of the canvas in the sewing. When the design is completed, the basting stitches are removed, and the horizontal and then the vertical threads of the canvas are removed, one strand at a time, with a tweezers. The cross-stitch design will remain on the fabric.

Although a background color is indicated for each design, bear in mind that in counted cross-stitch you do not have to work the background.

After you have completed your embroidery, wash it in cool or lukewarm water with a mild soap. Rinse well. Do not wring. Roll in a towel to remove excess moisture. Immediately iron on a padded surface with the embroidery face down. Be sure the embroidery is completely dry before attempting to mount.

To mount as a picture, center the embroidery over a pure white, rag-content mat board. Turn margins over the back evenly. Lace the margins with button thread, top to bottom, side to side. The fabric should be tight and even, with a little tension. Never use glue for mounting. Counted cross-stitch on cotton or linen may be framed under glass. Wool needs to breathe and should not be framed under glass unless breathing space is left.

Charted designs can be worked in filet crochet or in duplicate stitch over the squares formed by the crocheted afghan stitch or knitted stockinette stitch. The patterns can also be knitted directly into the work by working with more than one color, as in Fair Isle knitting. The wool not in use is always stranded across the back of the work. When it has to be stranded over more than five stitches, it should be twisted around the wool in use on every third stitch, thus preventing long strands at the back of the work. When a number of colors are used, a method known as "motif knitting" is employed. In this method short lengths of wool are wound on bobbins, using a separate length for each color and twisting the colors where they meet to avoid gaps in the work, as in knitting argyle socks.

Your local needlework shop or department where you buy your materials will be happy to help you with any problems.

I should like to thank Irene Loescher and Kathleen Foy for their help in working the embroidery which appears on the covers of this book.

SIAMESE CAT WITH PANSIES.

- ■ Dark brown
- ◨ Medium brown
- ◪ Light brown
- ⊡ Cream
- ◪ Light blue
- ◣ Dark purple
- ⊠ Yellow
- ⊙ Black
- ☐ Green

RABBIT WITH MUSHROOMS

- ■ Dark charcoal
- ◎ Medium grey
- ◩ Light grey
- ◧ Dark pink
- ⊠ Light pink
- ☐ White
- ⊡ Pale orange
- ◣ Dark orange
- ◪ Light orange
- ☐ Light blue

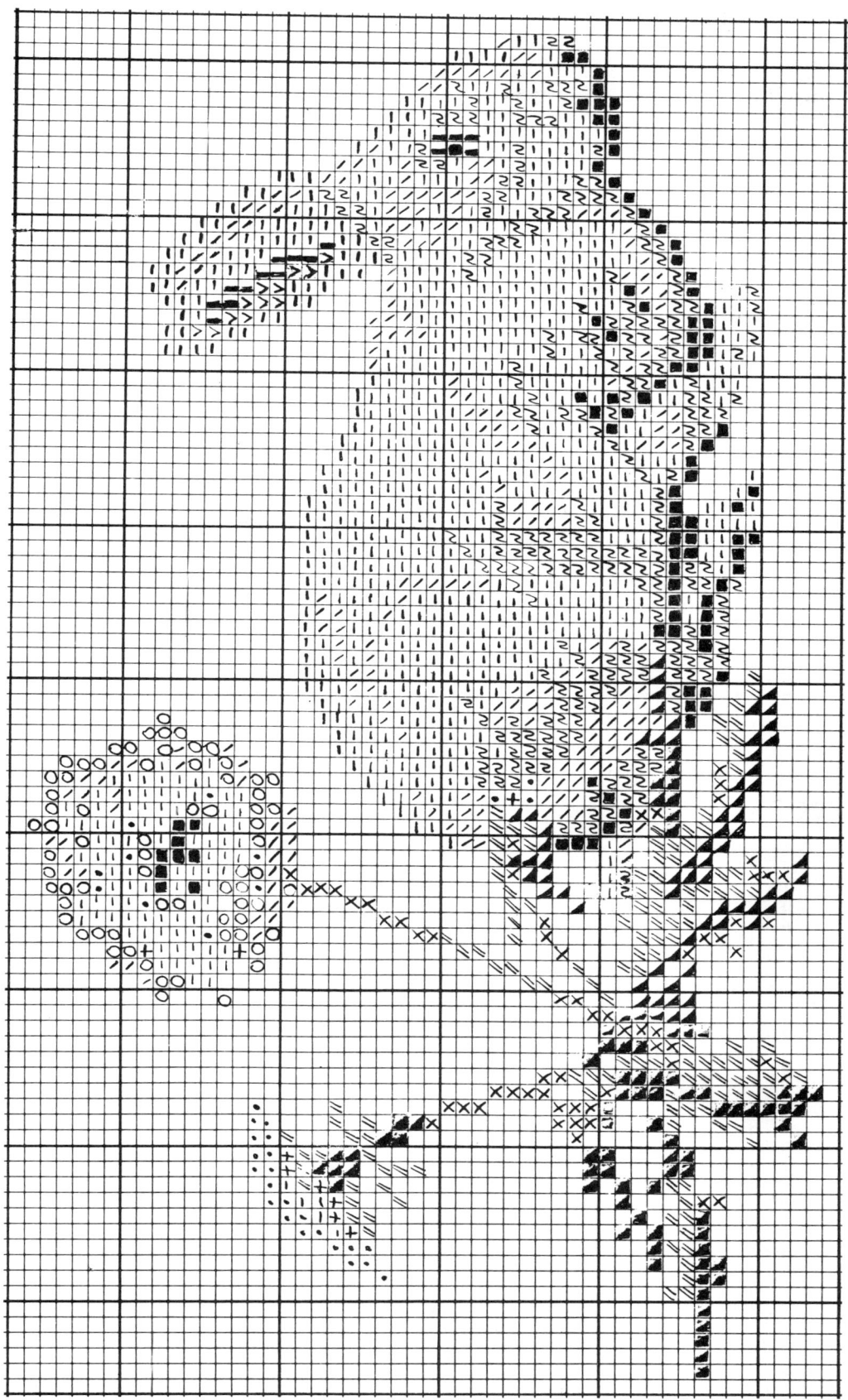

RABBIT WITH DANDELION

- ■ Dark charcoal
- ▨ Medium grey
- ▱ Light grey
- ◣ Dark green
- ▨ Medium green
- ▨ Light green
- ⊞ Dark yellow
- ⊡ Light yellow
- ■ Dark pink
- ▽ Light pink
- ◉ Ecru
- ☐ White
- ☐ Light blue

3

CANARIES WITH MORNING GLORIES

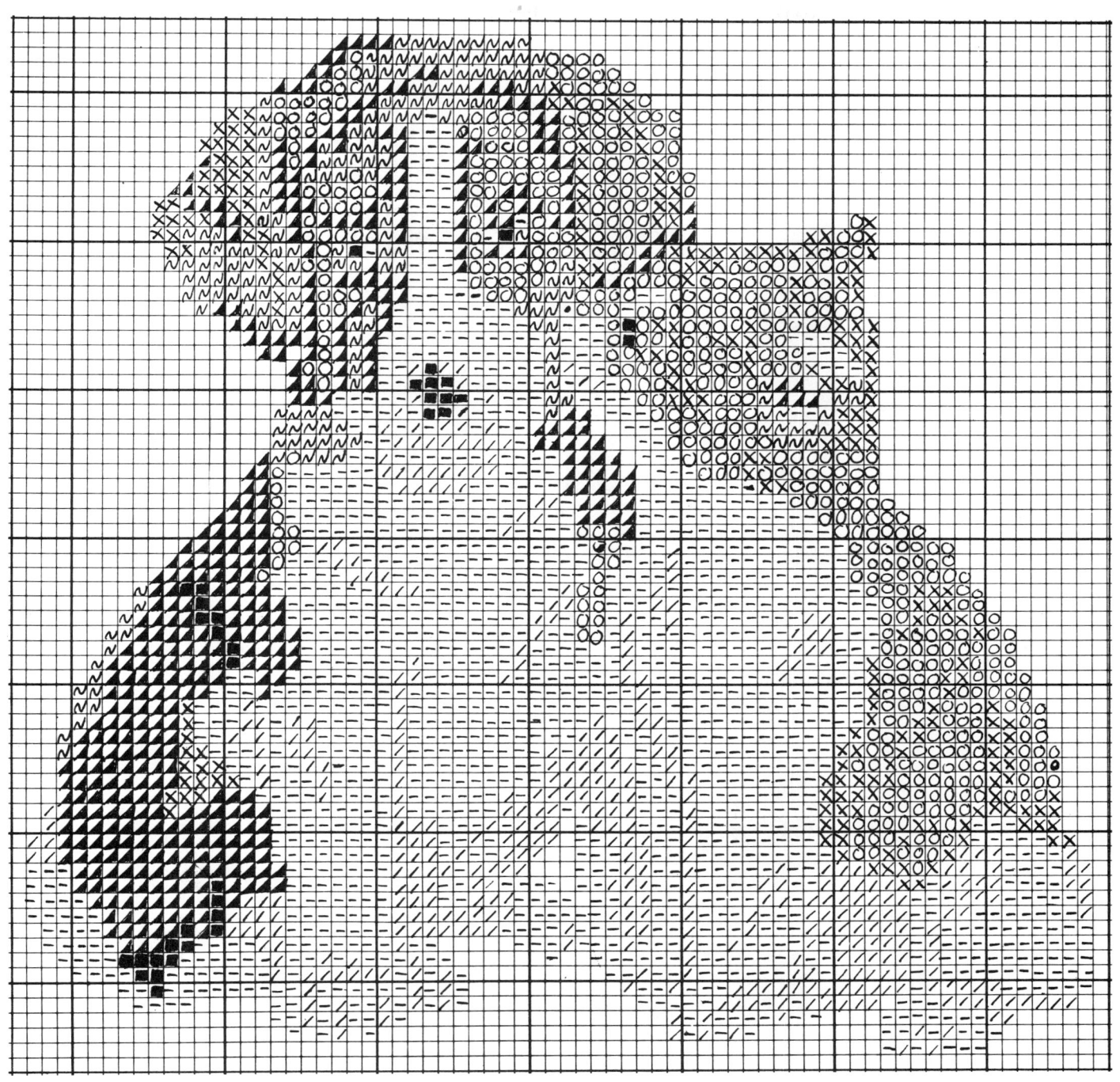

PUPPY AND KITTEN

◼ Dark brown ⊙ Gold ■ Black
∽ Light brown ⊠ Grey ⊡ Pink
⊠ Rust ⊟ White ☐ Blue

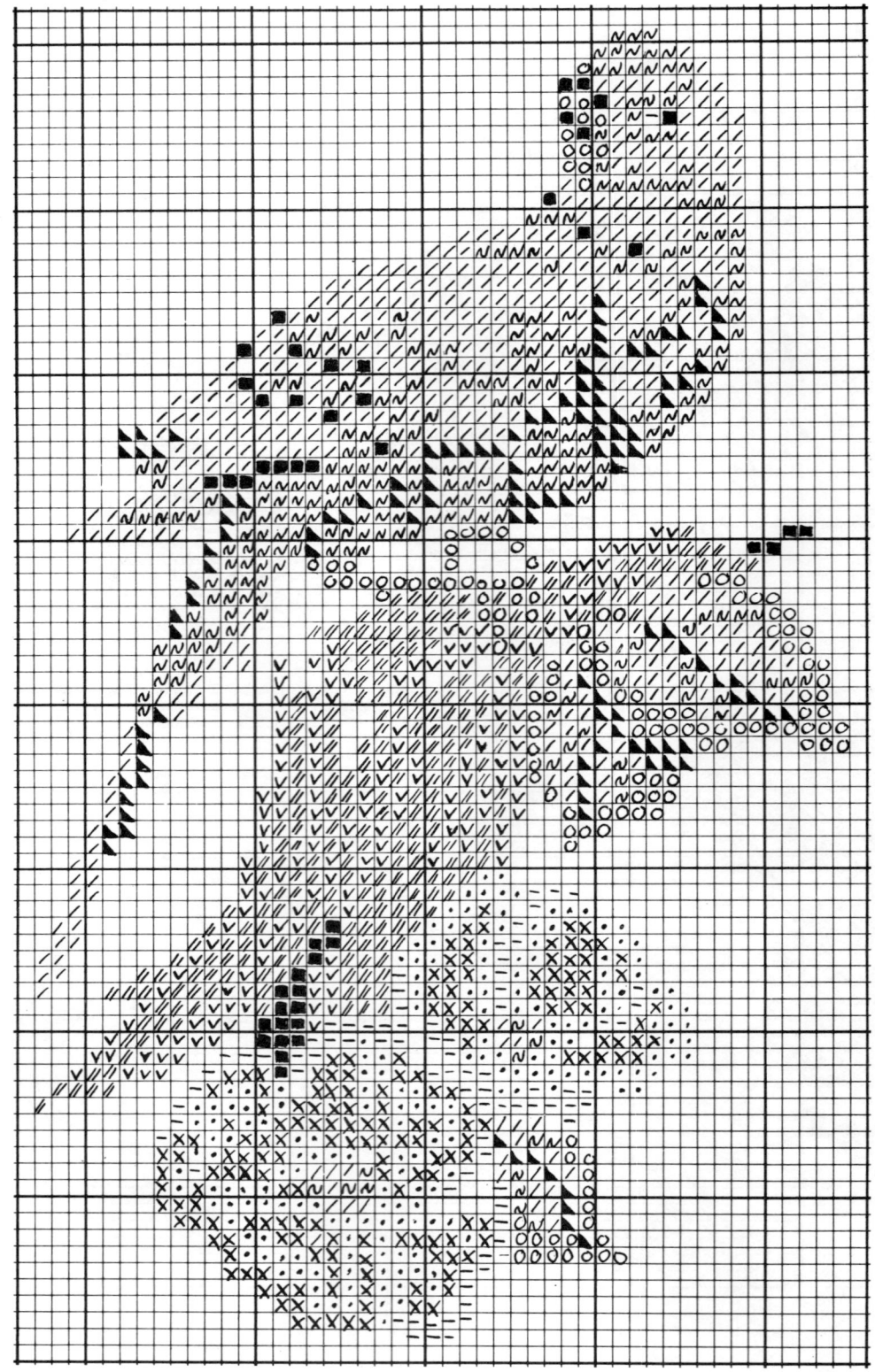

PARAKEET WITH MAGNOLIAS

- ■ Black
- ◣ Dark yellow-green
- Ⓝ Medium yellow-green
- ╱ Light yellow-green
- ⋁ Medium brown
- ⊘ Light brown
- ⊠ Dark pale pink
- ⊙ Light pale pink
- ⊟ White
- ⊙ Gold
- ☐ Dark brown

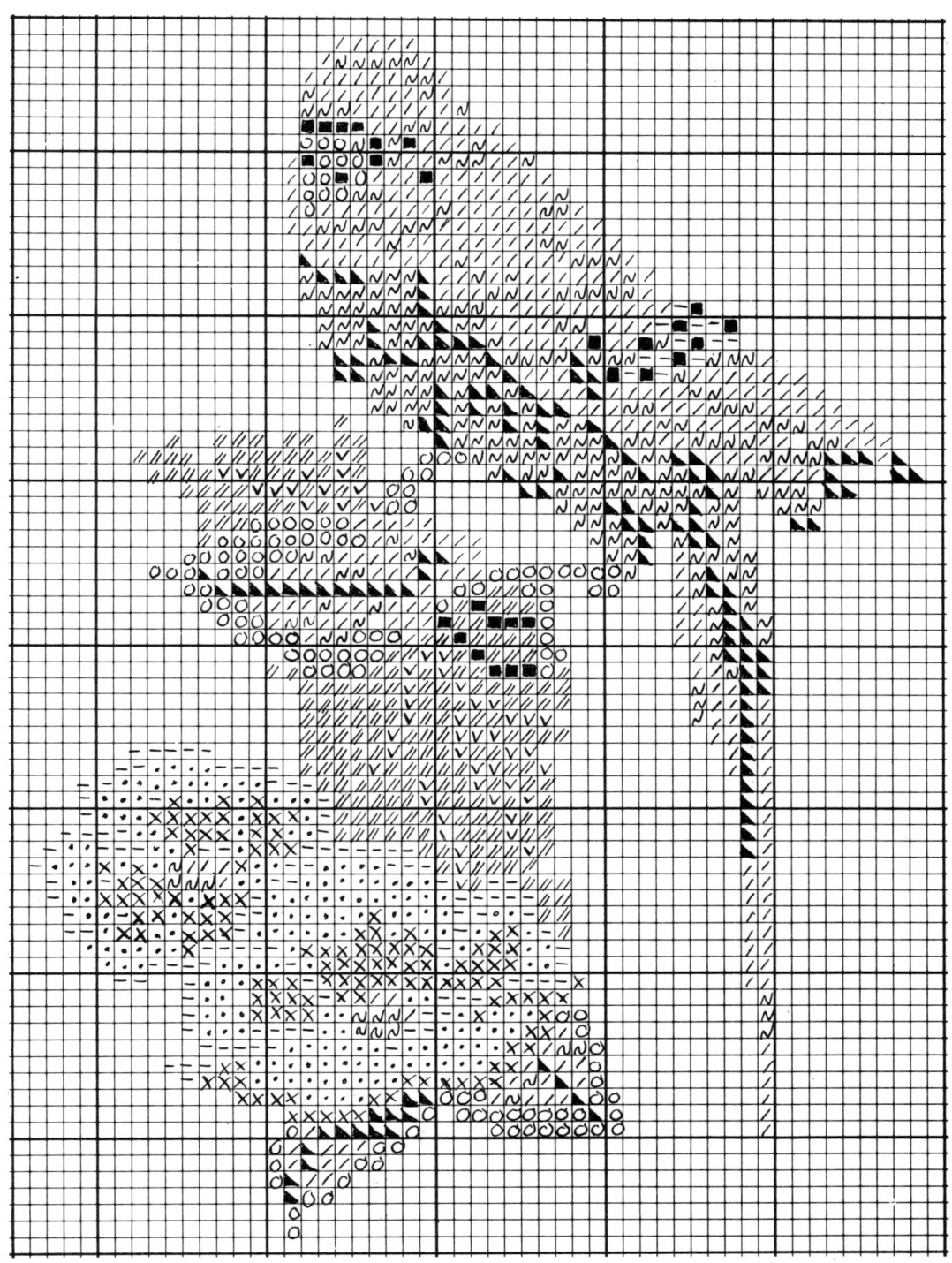

PARAKEET WITH MAGNOLIAS

◼ Black ⱱ Medium brown ⊟ White
◣ Dark turquoise ⊡ Light brown ⊙ Gold
Ⱨ Medium turquoise ⊠ Dark pale pink ☐ Dark brown
⊘ Light turquoise ⊙ Light pale pink

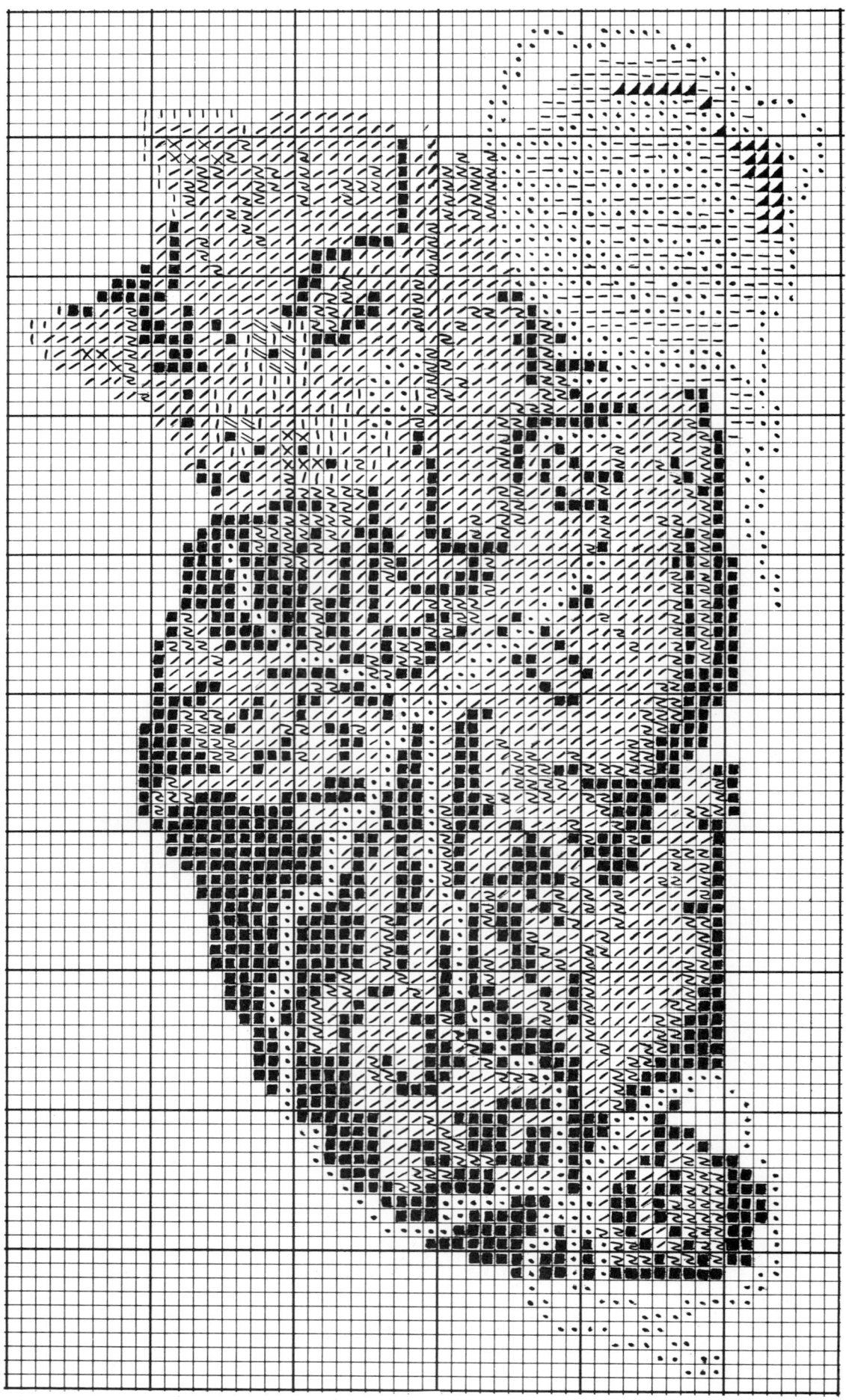

KITTEN WITH YARN

- ■ Dark grey
- ☒ Medium grey
- ╱ Light grey
- ☐ White
- ◣ Dark blue
- ▬ Medium blue
- • Light blue
- ☒ Green
- ☒ Pink
- ☐ Yellow

KITTEN PREENING

- ■ Black
- ◨ Grey
- ⊟ White
- ⊡ Light pink
- ⊿ Medium pink
- ☐ Red

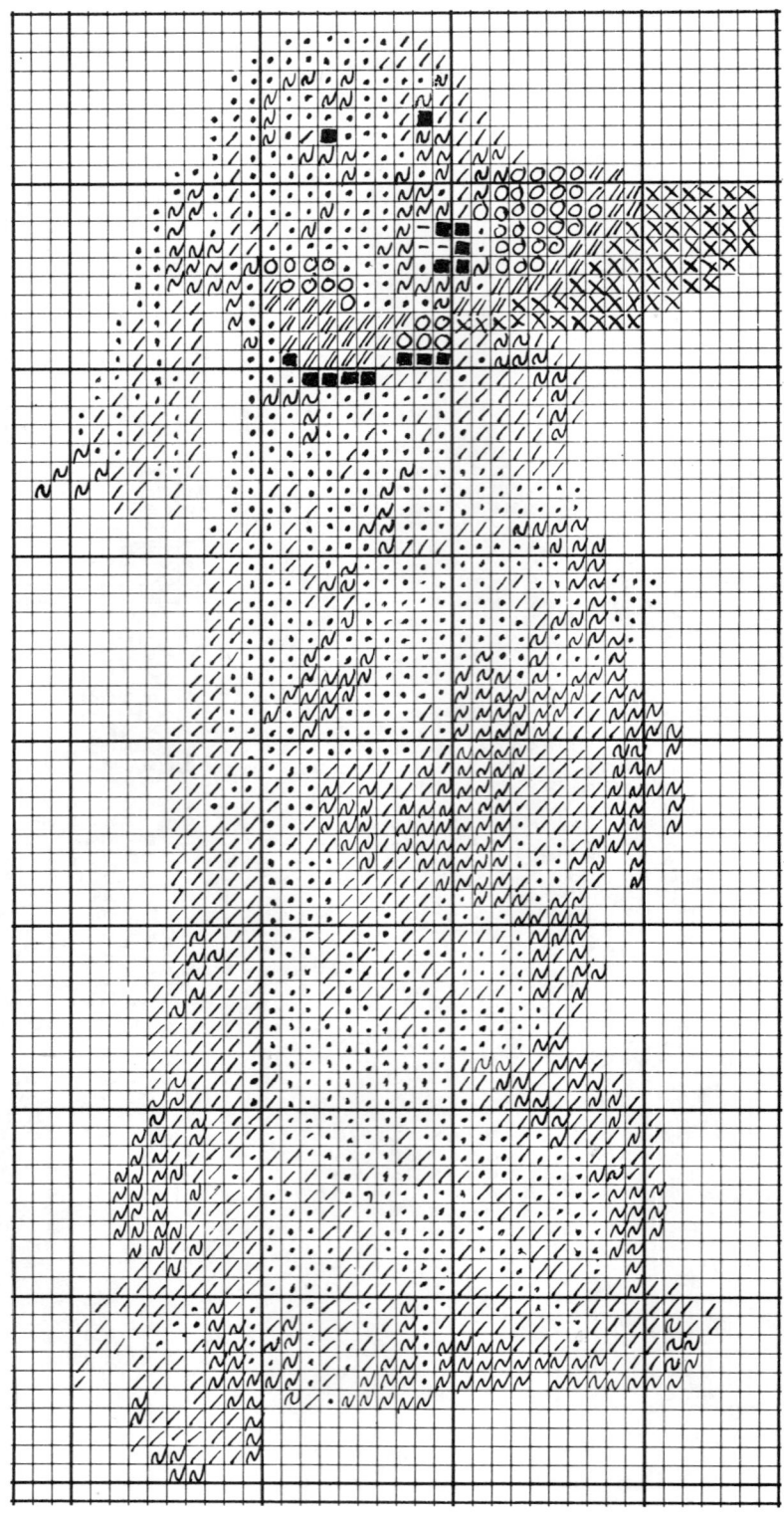

DOG WITH SLIPPER

- ■ Black
- ◫ Dark rust
- ⟋ Medium rust
- · Light rust
- ⊠ Light blue
- ⟋ Yellow
- ⊙ Pink
- ⊟ White
- ☐ Light green

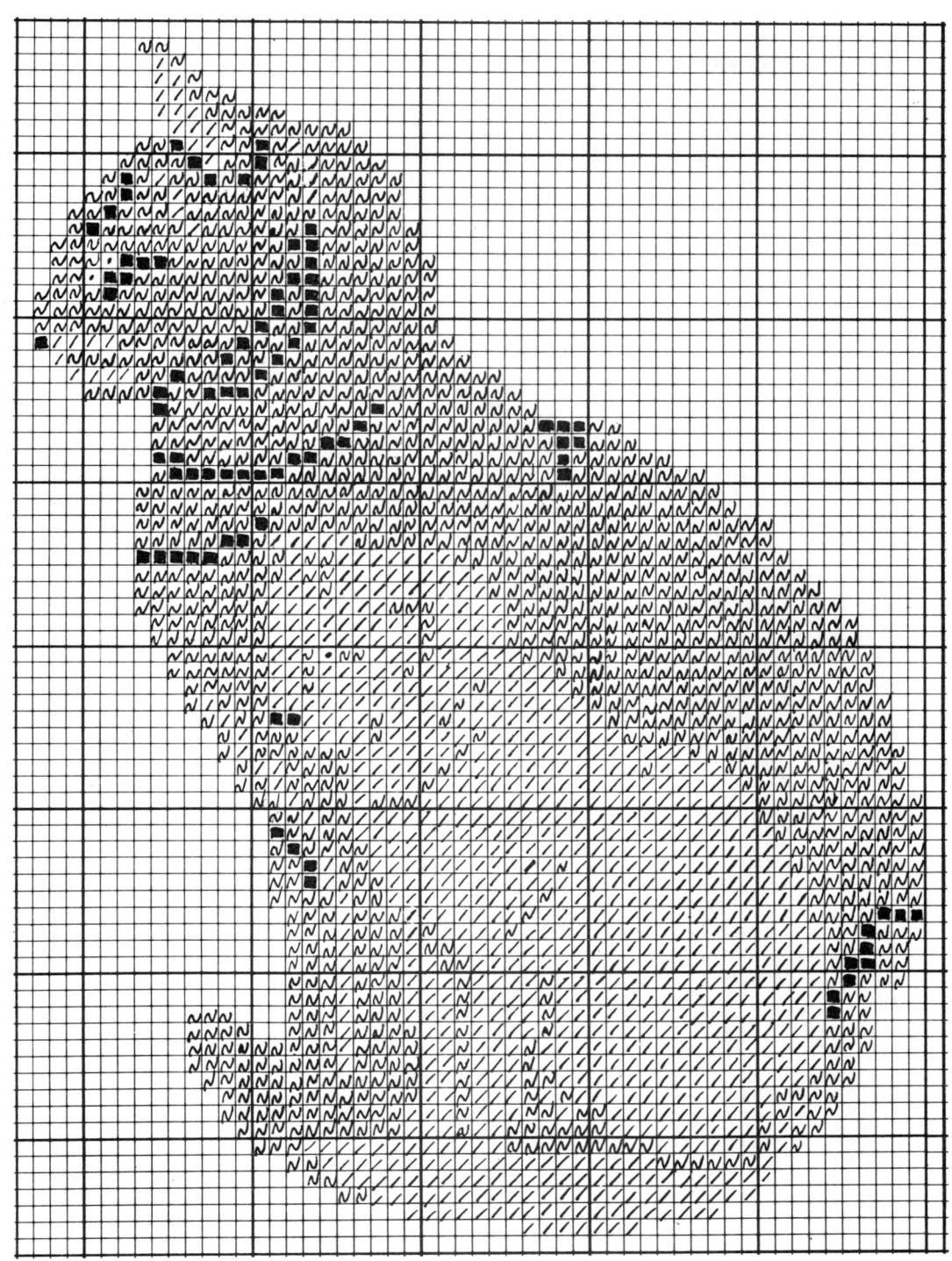

CAT WITH KITTEN

■ Rust ◨ Amber
◨ Cream ☐ Light blue
⊡ Yellow

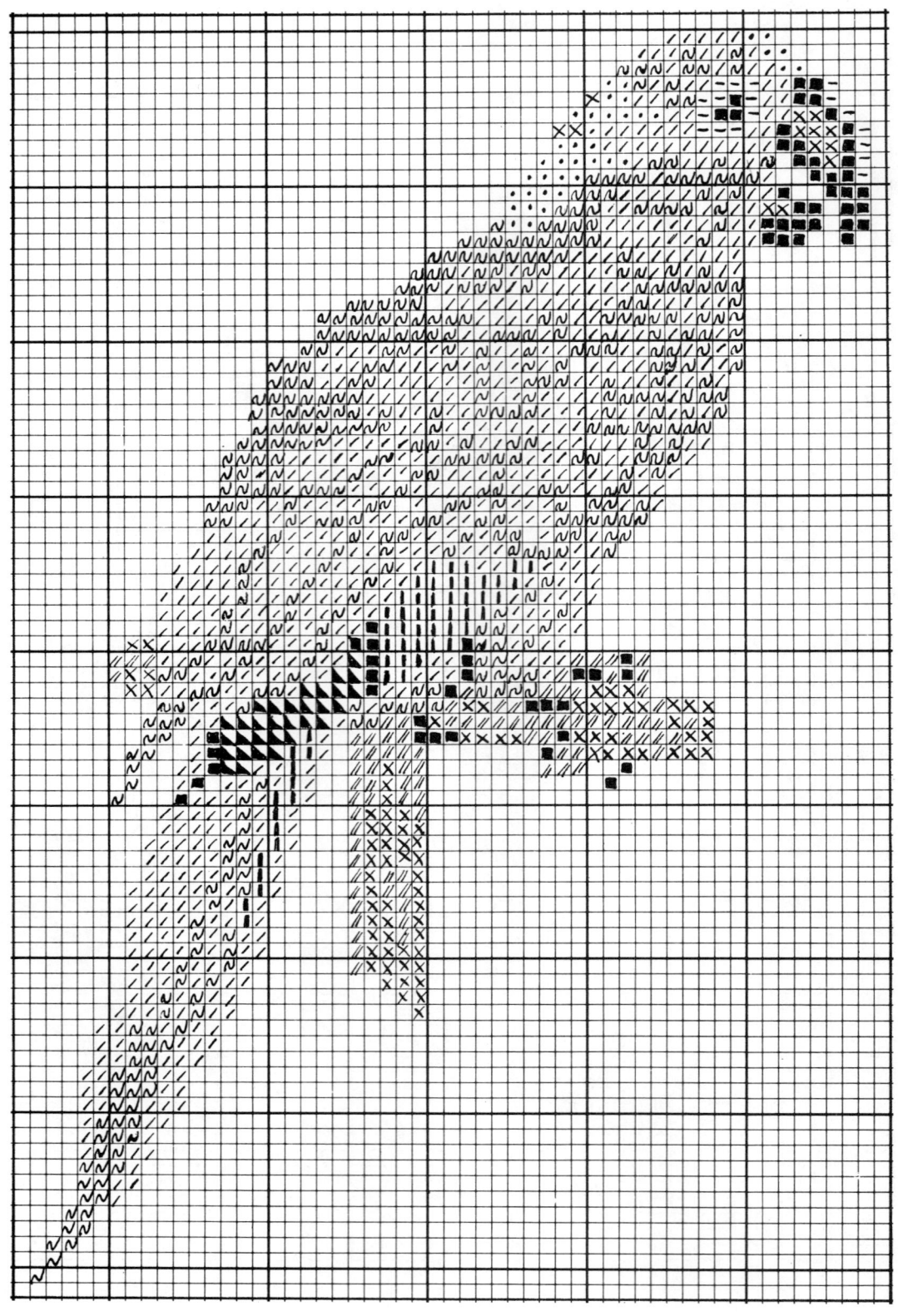

PARROT

- ■ Black
- ⊠ Dark green
- ∕ Light green
- · Yellow
- Ⅱ Red
- ◣ Blue
- ⊠ Dark brown
- ⊠ Light brown
- ⊟ White
- ☐ Beige

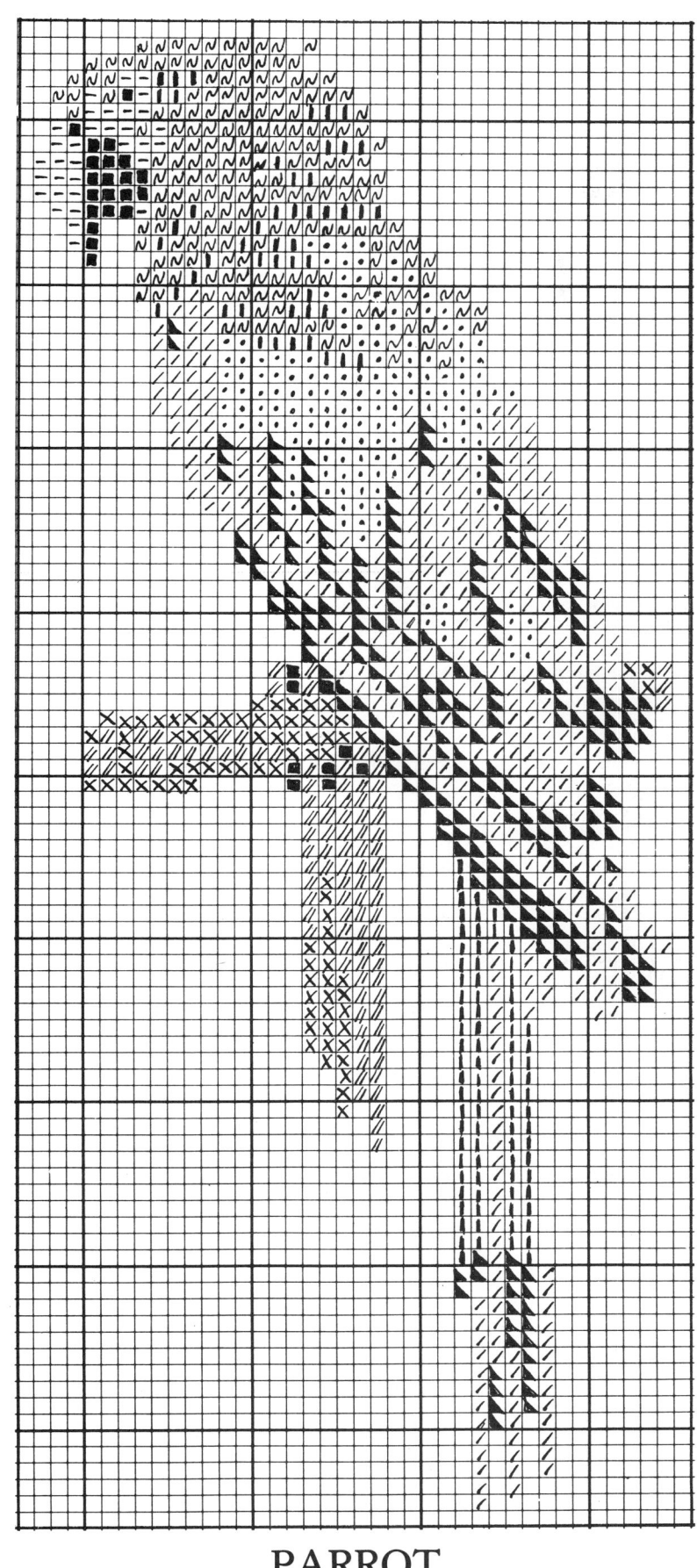

PARROT

- ■ Black
- ⊟ White
- ⊠ Red
- ⓘ Dark red
- ⊡ Green
- ◣ Dark blue
- ☐ Light blue
- ⧄ Dark brown
- ⊠ Light brown
- ☐ Beige

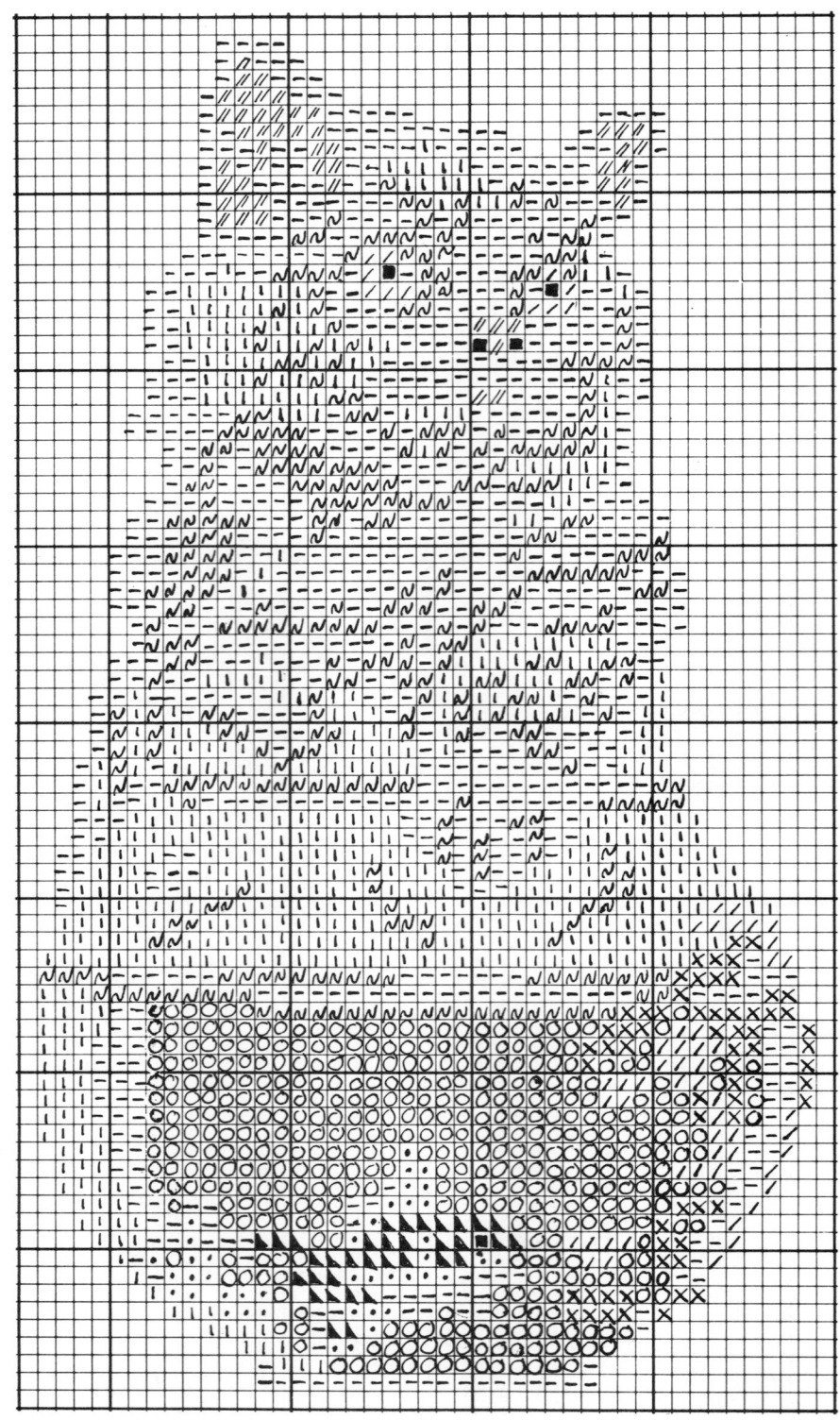

KITTEN WITH GOLDFISH

- ■ Black
- ⊠ Dark green
- ⊘ Pink
- ⊌ Medium grey
- ⊘ Medium green
- ● Gold
- ⊡ Light grey
- ⊙ Light green
- ☐ Turquoise
- ⊟ White
- ◤ Dark orange

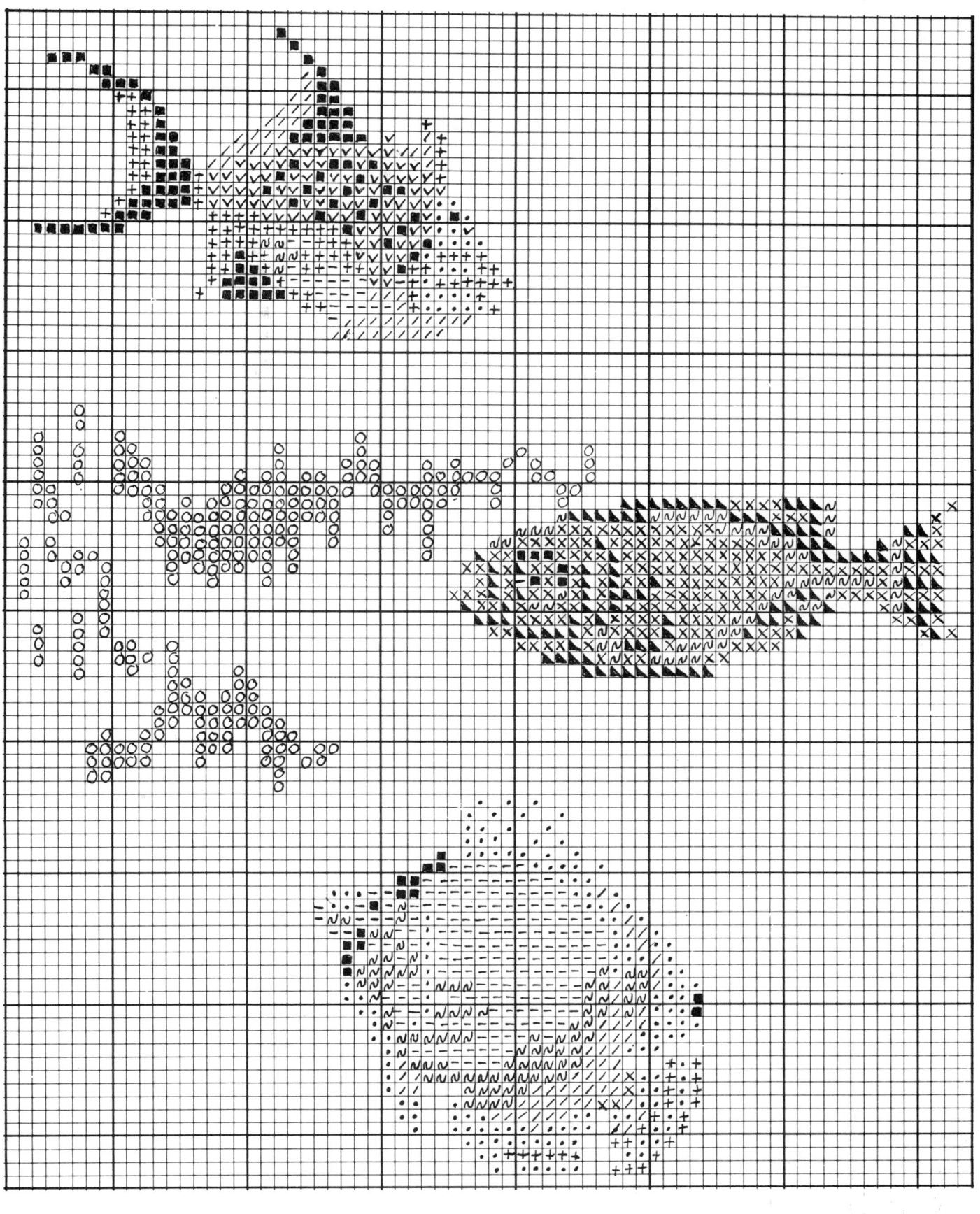

TROPICAL FISH

| ■ Black | ⊟ White | ⊘ Dark yellow | ⊽ Yellow-green | ⊠ Light orange | ▢ Medium green |
| ⊡ Grey | ⊞ Turquoise | ⊡ Light yellow | ◣ Dark orange | ⊙ Dark green | |

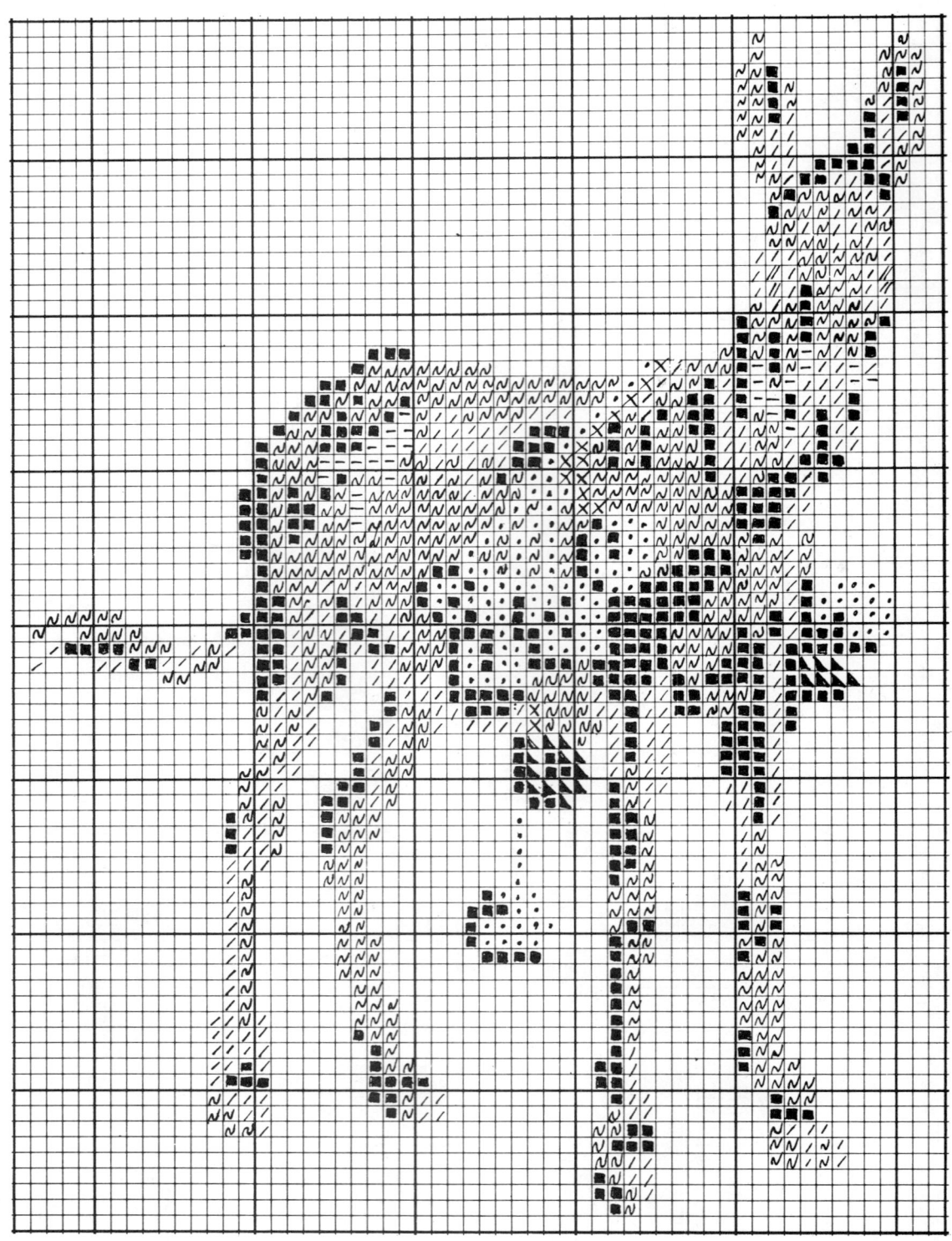

DONKEY

■ Dark grey   ⊟ White   ◣ Blue
ɷ Medium grey ⊠ Brown   ⊠ Gold
⁄ Light grey   ⊡ Red   ☐ Cream

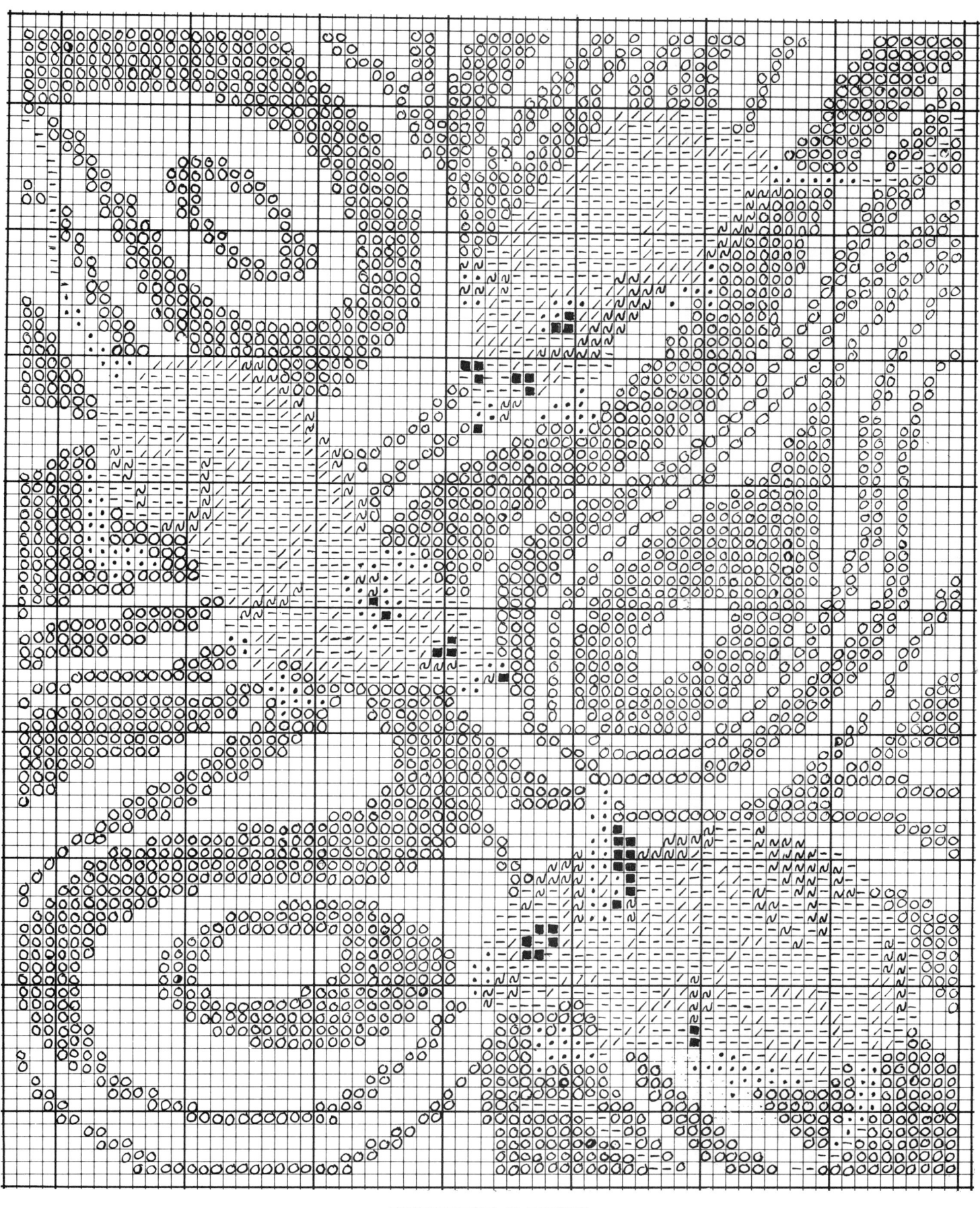

WHITE MICE

■ Black   ◨ Dark grey   ⁄ Light grey   · Light pink   ◉ Red   ☐ Bright pink

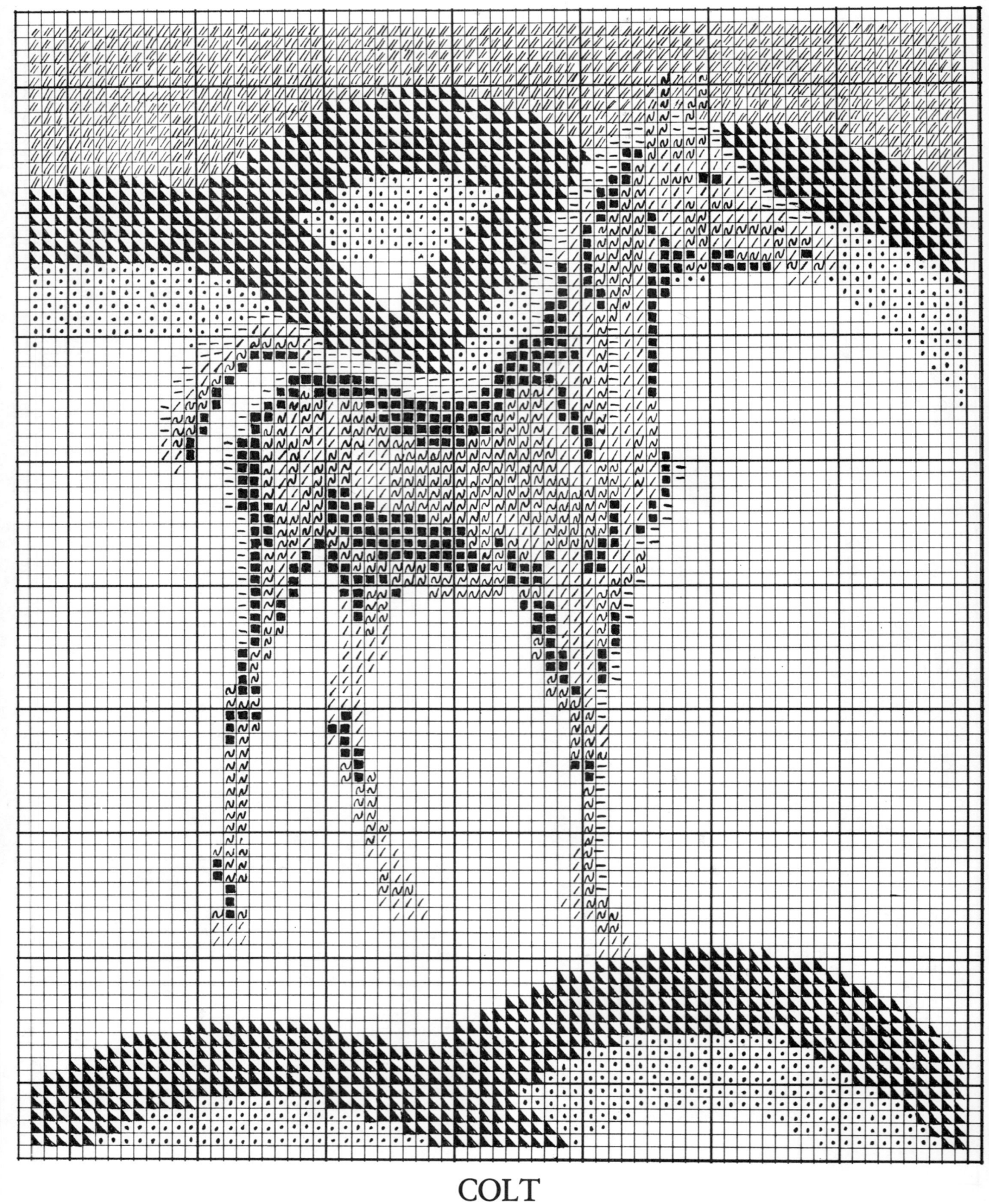

COLT

- ■ Black
- ☑ Light grey
- ◣ Dark green
- ⊘ Blue
- ɴ Dark grey
- ⊟ White
- ⊡ Medium green
- ☐ Light green

COLT

■ Dark brown   ⊘ Light brown   ◣ Dark green   ⊘ Blue
∾ Medium brown   ⊟ White   · Medium green   ☐ Light green

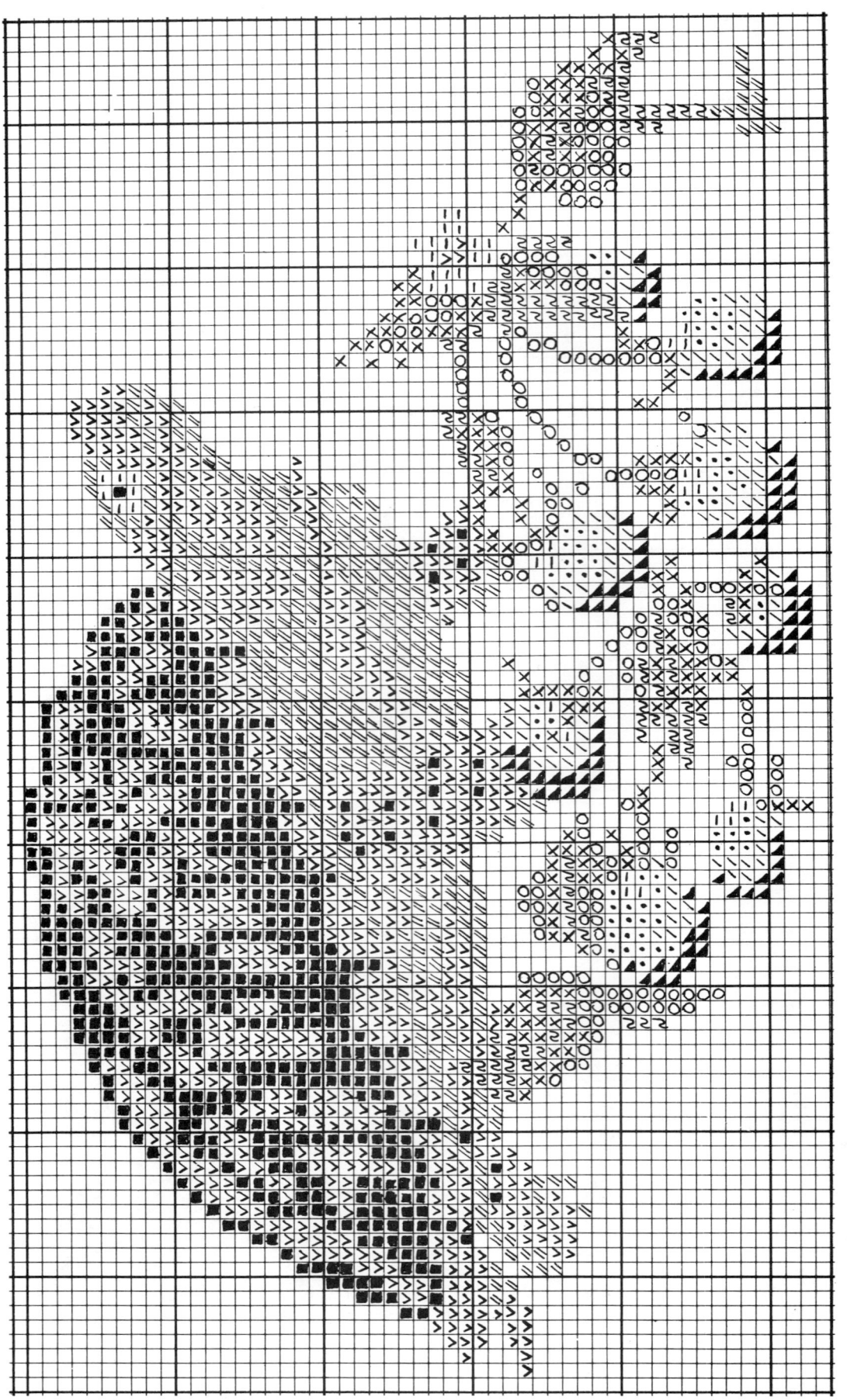

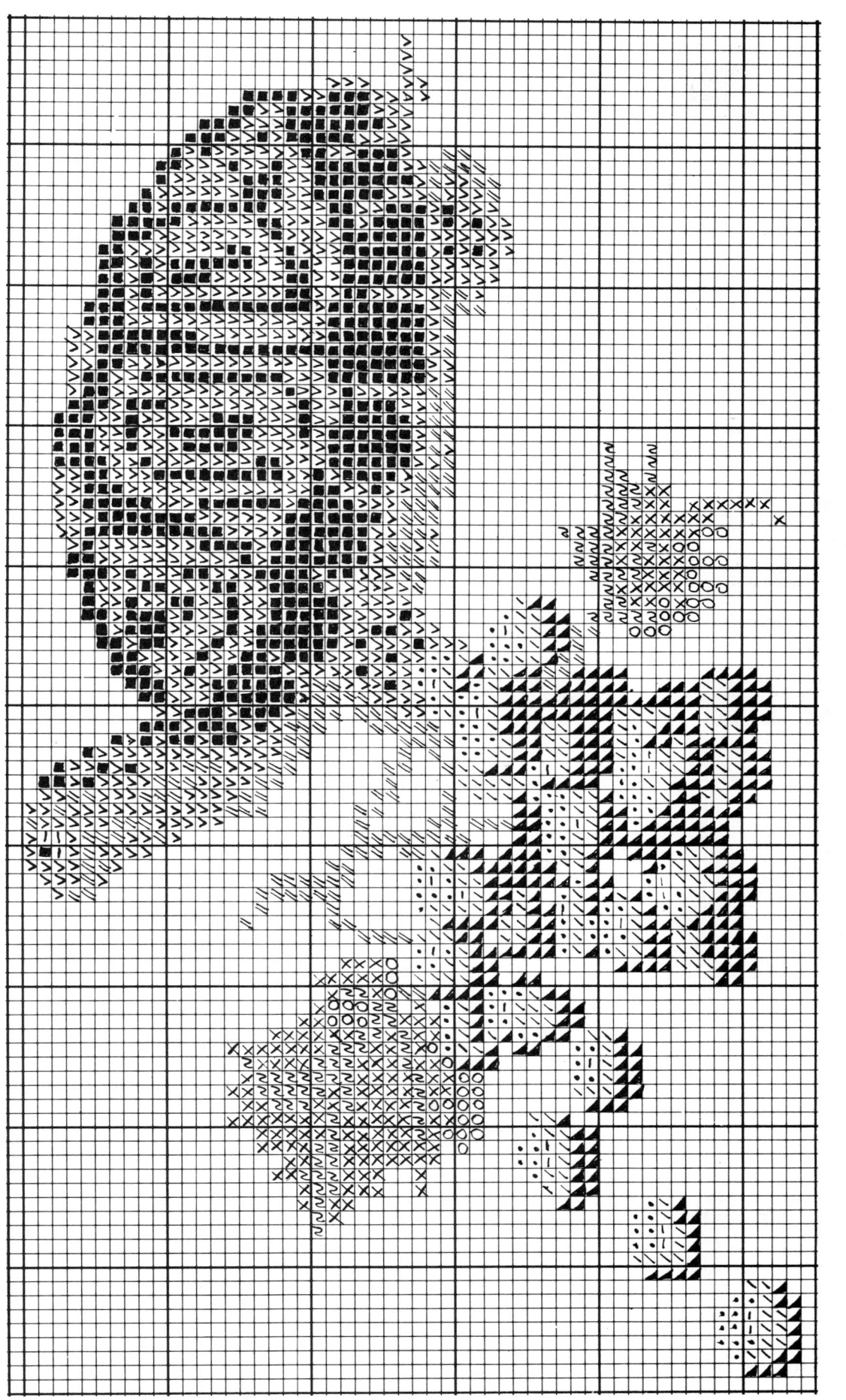

TURTLE WITH GRAPES

- ■ Dark blue
- ▷ Gold
- □ White
- ▨ Dark green
- ⊡ Medium green
- ⊙ Light green
- ◪ Dark grape
- ▨ Medium grape
- ⊡ Light grape
- ⊠ Brown
- □ Light blue

21

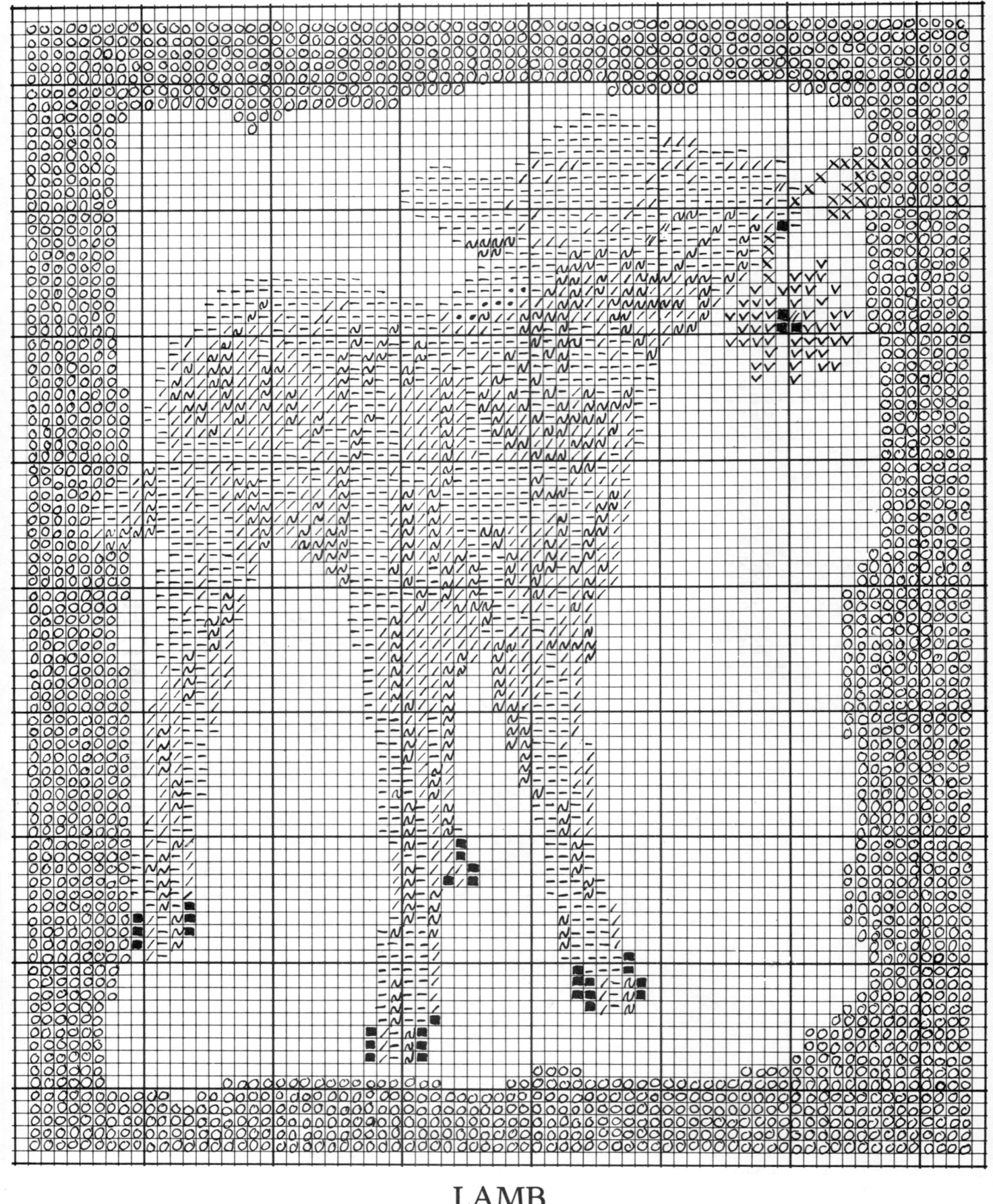

LAMB

■ Black　　☑ Light grey　　⊟ White　　⊠ Green　　⊡ Deep melon
@ Dark grey　　⊡ Pink　　☒ Brown　　☒ Yellow　　☐ Light melon

MORE CHARTED DESIGN BOOKS FROM DOVER

CHARTED DESIGNS FOR NEEDLE-MADE RUGS, Sibyl I. Mathews. 45 charted designs ready to transfer onto rug canvas: dolphins, tulips, toy soldiers, Manx motifs, many more. Full instructions; 44 additional illustrations. 150pp. 7⅞ x 10¾. 23264-6 Pa. **$4.00**

CHARTED PEASANT DESIGNS FROM SAXON TRANSYLVANIA, Heinz E. Kiewe. 195 authentic cross-stitch designs, 11th through early 20th century. Birds, flowers, geometric patterns, mythical beasts, more. Detailed introduction identifies symbols, patterns. 64pp. 8¼ x 11. 23425-8 Pa. **$2.00**

A TREASURY OF CHARTED DESIGNS FOR NEEDLEWORKERS, Georgia L. Gorham and Jeanne M. Warth. 141 motifs charted for ready use include lovebirds, cat with yarn, toy train, pansies, windmill, etc. Designs most prized by needleworkers. Instructions. Color key. 48pp. 8¼ x 11. 23558-0 Pa. **$1.75**

CHARTED MONOGRAMS FOR NEEDLEPOINT AND CROSS-STITCH, Rita Weiss. 350 striking turn-of-the-century monograms, taken from a rare Viennese album. Also includes many crowns, complete sets of Roman and Arabic numerals. 48pp. 8¼ x 11. 23555-6 Pa. **$1.95**

CHARTED SWISS FOLK DESIGNS, Elvira Parolini-Ruffini. Lovely charted versions of crowns, stars, flowers, hunting scenes, etc., collected from the Engadine Valley in the Swiss canton of Grisons. Magnificent folk art. 32pp. 8¼ x 11. (Available in U.S. only) 23574-2 Pa. **$1.50**

CLASSIC POSTERS FOR NEEDLEPOINT, Elizabeth Irvine. 22 classic art posters by Mucha, Will Bradley, the Beggarstaffs, charted for any variety of needlepoint. Yarn and canvas requirements, authentic color schemes provided. 48pp. 8¼ x 11. 23640-4 Pa. **$1.75**

NEEDLEPOINT DESIGNS AFTER ILLUSTRATIONS BY BEATRIX POTTER, Rita Weiss. 24 popular Beatrix Potter scenes, characters charted for needlepoint or counted thread embroidery. All reproduced in full-color needlepoint on covers. 32pp. 8¼ x 11. (Available in U.S. only) 20218-6 Pa. **$1.75**

CHRISTMAS NEEDLEPOINT DESIGNS, Rita Weiss. 36 original seasonal designs including 12 Days of Christmas series. Graphed for ready transfer onto # 10 needlepoint canvas. Instructions for gift projects. 36 cover illustrations. 32pp. 8¼ x 11. 23161-5 Pa. **$1.50**

BAROQUE CHARTED DESIGNS FOR NEEDLEWORK, Johan Sibmacher. 36 plates reprinted from 1604 Nuremberg needlework patterns. All graphed. Geometrics, heraldic, mythological and religious designs. 99 motifs total. 48pp. 8¼ x 11. 23186-0 Pa. **$1.75**

PERSIAN RUG MOTIFS FOR NEEDLEPOINT CHARTED FOR EASY USE, Lyatif Kerimov. 160 motifs from Russian-Iranian borderlands. Birds, florals, animals, border designs, more, in traditional renderings. 45 plates. 48pp. 8¼ x 11. 23187-9 Pa. **$2.00**

AFRICAN NEEDLEPOINT DESIGNS CHARTED FOR EASY USE, Diana Oliver Turner. 45 designs based on the rich African art tradition: masks, animals, birds, geometrics, etc. Charted for easy use in needlepoint or counted thread embroidery. 25 color illustrations altogether. 41pp. 8¼ x 11. 23244-1 Pa. **$2.00**

PENNSYLVANIA DUTCH NEEDLEPOINT DESIGNS CHARTED FOR EASY USE, Marcia Loeb. 50 authentic designs suitable for pillows, belts, pictures, etc. All charted for easy use in needlepoint and counted thread embroidery. 22 designs rendered in full-color needlepoint on covers. 48pp. 8¼ x 11. 23299-9 Pa. **$1.95**

NEEDLEWORK ALPHABETS AND DESIGNS, edited by Blanche Cirker. 27 alphabets, many geometric designs, animals, butterflies, pictorial materials printed in 2 colors on grids for easy use. Dillmont material, very beautiful. 85pp. (Available in U.S. only) 23159-3 Pa. **$2.50**

GEOMETRIC NEEDLEPOINT DESIGNS, Carol Belanger Grafton. 43 imaginative charted designs, all original, produce striking color effects, op art, even visual illusions. 16 color designs on covers. Instructions. 41pp. 8¼ x 11. 23160-7 Pa. **$1.75**

FAVORITE ILLUSTRATIONS FROM CHILDREN'S CLASSICS IN COUNTED CROSS-STITCH, Ginnie Thompson. Famous needlewoman offers 28 sewing pictures from Tenniel's *Alice*, Denslow's *Wizard of Oz*, Kate Greenaway. 42pp. 8¼ x 11. 23394-4 Pa. **$1.75**

PATCHWORK QUILT DESIGNS FOR NEEDLEPOINT CHARTED FOR EASY USE, Frank Fontana. 41 traditional quilt block patterns selected and adapted; capture early American flavor, striking modern effects. Full general directions. Historical captions. Each charted on 7½ x 7½-inch square. Repeat or combine for almost any size project. 48pp. 8¼ x 11. 23300-6 Pa. **$1.95**

FULL-COLOR AMERICAN INDIAN DESIGNS FOR NEEDLEPOINT RUGS CHARTED FOR EASY USE, Dorothy Story. 32 plates of authentic material, all in full color; charted for # 5 canvas, but also other applications. Pillows, rugs, hangings, etc. 32pp. 8¼ x 11. 23190-9 Pa. **$2.00**

FULL-COLOR FLORAL NEEDLEPOINT DESIGNS CHARTED FOR EASY USE, Eva Costabel-Deutsch. Startling oversized blooms, delicate sprays, intriguing bouquetlike combinations, and Art Deco elaborations of floral motifs: 32 designs in full, vibrant colors, charted for easy use on # 10 needlepoint canvas. 32pp. 8¼ x 11. 23387-1 Pa. **$2.50**

AMERICAN INDIAN NEEDLEPOINT DESIGNS FOR PILLOWS, BELTS, HANDBAGS AND OTHER PROJECTS, Roslyn Epstein. 37 authentic American Indian designs adapted for modern needlepoint projects. Grid backing makes designs easily transferable to canvas. 48pp. 8¼ x 11. 22973-4 Pa. **$1.50**

VICTORIAN NEEDLEPOINT DESIGNS FROM GODEY'S LADY'S BOOK AND PETERSON'S MAGAZINE, Godey's Lady's Book. Edited by Rita Weiss. Unique, remarkable pictorial needlepoint, on grids, from finest sources: 43 in all, bicyclists, cats, horses, sea scenes, dancers, overall designs, etc. Instructions. 36pp. 8¼ x 11. 23163-1 Pa. **$2.00**

FULL-COLOR BICENTENNIAL NEEDLEPOINT DESIGNS, Carol Belanger Grafton. 32 full-color charted designs: slogans and flags, portrait of Washington, minuteman and drummer boy, cannon, Paul Revere's ride, other patriotic designs inspired by the Bicentennial. Full instructions. 32pp. in full color. 8¼ x 11. 23233-6 Pa. **$2.00**

FULL-COLOR RUSSIAN FOLK NEEDLEPOINT DESIGNS CHARTED FOR EASY USE, Frieda Halpern. 31 full-page, full-color designs are adapted from Russian folk designs. Elegant yet child-like riders on horseback, mythical beasts, birds, florals, geometric patterns. Charted for easy use on # 10 needlepoint canvas. Instructions. 32pp. 8¼ x 11. 23451-7 Pa. **$2.95**

CHARTED FOLK DESIGNS FOR CROSS-STITCH EMBROIDERY, Maria Foris & Andreas Foris. 278 charted folk designs, most in 2 colors, from Danube region: florals, fantastic beasts, geometrics, traditional symbols, more. Border and central patterns. 77pp. 8¼ x 11. 23191-7 Pa. **$2.95**

ANNE ORR'S CHARTED DESIGNS, Anne Orr. Over 100 best designs by premier needlework designer, all on charts: flowers, borders, birds, children, alphabets, etc. Widely bought 1910 to 1945, still sought after today. Over 100 charts, 10 in color, and 7 photos. Total of 40pp. 8¼ x 11. 23704-4 Pa. **$2.00**

Paperbound unless otherwise indicated. Prices subject to change without notice. Available at your book dealer or write for free catalogues to Dept. Needlework 15, Dover Publications Inc., 180 Varick St., N.Y., N.Y. 10014. Please indicate your field of interest. Each year Dover publishes over 150 books on music, fine art, science, languages, chess, puzzles, nature, anthropology, antiques, folklore, art instruction, crafts, needlework, and other areas.

Manufactured in the U.S.A.